-id as in squid

Kelly Doudna

Consulting Editor Monica Marx, M.A./Reading Specialist

ABDO
Publishing Company

Published by SandCastle™, an imprint of ABDO Publishing Company, 4940 Viking Drive, Edina, Minnesota 55435.

Printed in the United States.

Credits
Edited by: Pam Price
Curriculum Coordinator: Nancy Tuminelly
Cover and Interior Design and Production: Mighty Media
Photo Credits: BananaStock Ltd., Corel, Eyewire Images, Hemera, PhotoDisc

Library of Congress Cataloging-in-Publication Data

Doudna, Kelly, 1963-
-Id as in squid / Kelly Doudna.
    p. cm. -- (Word families. Set III)
    Summary: Introduces, in brief text and illustrations, the use of the letter combination "id" in such words as "squid," "lid," "grid," and "pyramid."
    ISBN 1-59197-235-3
    1. Readers (Primary) [1. Vocabulary. 2. Reading.] I. Title.

PE1119 .D67583 2003
428.1--dc21   2002038632

SandCastle™ books are created by a professional team of educators, reading specialists, and content developers around five essential components that include phonemic awareness, phonics, vocabulary, text comprehension, and fluency. All books are written, reviewed, and leveled for guided reading, early intervention reading, and Accelerated Reader® programs and designed for use in shared, guided, and independent reading and writing activities to support a balanced approach to literacy instruction.

Let Us Know

After reading the book, SandCastle would like you to tell us your stories about reading. What is your favorite page? Was there something hard that you needed help with? Share the ups and downs of learning to read. We want to hear from you! To get posted on the ABDO Publishing Company Web site, send us e-mail at:

sandcastle@abdopub.com

SandCastle Level: Beginning

-id Words

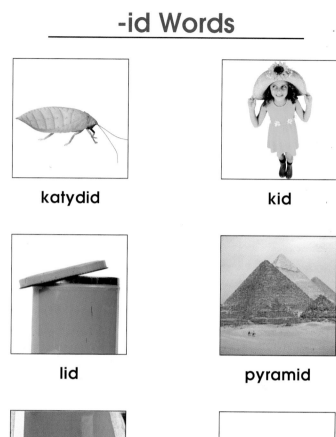

katydid

kid

lid

pyramid

slid

squid

3

A katydid sits on a leaf.

Ling plays with another kid.

The lid is next to the
cookie jar.

A pyramid looks like
a triangle.

Sid slid into the water.

A squid lives in the ocean.

10

The Squid and the Kid

The kid saw a squid.

The squid hid
under a lid.

The squid
surprised the kid.

The kid
rubbed each eyelid.

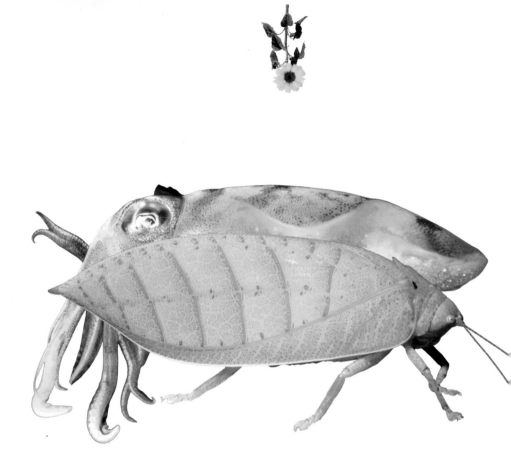

The squid hid
behind a katydid.

The squid hid
behind a pyramid.

The squid slid.

20

At last the kid
was rid of the squid.

The -id Word Family

bid	lid
did	pyramid
eyelid	rid
grid	Sid
hid	skid
katydid	slid
kid	squid

Glossary

Some of the words in this list may have more than one meaning. The meaning listed here reflects the way the word is used in the book.

katydid   a green insect related to grasshoppers and crickets

lid   the top or cover of a container

pyramid   an Egyptian monument that is square on the bottom with four sides shaped like triangles

squid   a sea animal with a soft body and ten tentacles around the mouth

triangle   a shape with three straight sides

About SandCastle™

A professional team of educators, reading specialists, and content developers created the SandCastle™ series to support young readers as they develop reading skills and strategies and increase their general knowledge. The SandCastle™ series has four levels that correspond to early literacy development in young children. The levels are provided to help teachers and parents select the appropriate books for young readers.

Emerging Readers
(no flags)

Beginning Readers
(1 flag)

Transitional Readers
(2 flags)

Fluent Readers
(3 flags)

These levels are meant only as a guide. All levels are subject to change.

To see a complete list of SandCastle™ books and other nonfiction titles from ABDO Publishing Company, visit www.abdopub.com or contact us at:

4940 Viking Drive, Edina, Minnesota 55435 • 1-800-800-1312 • fax: 1-952-831-1632